Writing Skills Builder

Level 1
English

First edition 2013

ISBN 978-981-07-3279-0

Welcome to studySMART!

Writing Skills Builder provides opportunities for the systematic development of your child's writing skills as he progresses from word to sentence to paragraph.

It is often a challenge to help children develop their writing skills. The high-interest topics and engaging exercises in this book will both stimulate and encourage your child to develop the necessary skills to become an independent writer. As your child encounters a variety of texts and language features, he will learn to select the appropriate language structures and plan, write and proofread his writing.

Every section targets a specific skill and there are two mini-projects that are appropriately placed to ensure that your child uses the skills he has picked up in previous sections.

How to use this book

1. Introduce the target writing skill at the top of the page to your child.

2. Direct his attention to the Note, where there is one, and go through the skills tip with your child.

3. Let your child complete the writing exercises.

4. Reinforce your child's learning with an extension activity at the end of each exercise. These activities provide additional practice, and extend your child's learning of the particular writing skill.

5. Refer to the Writing Tips section at the end of the book for a recap of some fundamental strategies to improve your child's writing.

Note: To avoid the awkward 'he or she' construction, the pronouns on this page and in the parents' note will refer to the male gender.

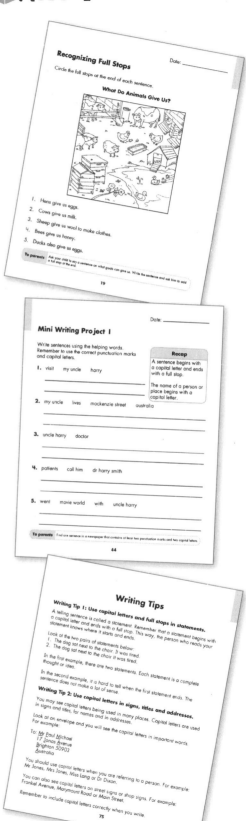

Contents

Recognizing Capital Letters

Help the mouse through the maze by coloring each box with a word that begins with a capital letter.

That's Amazing!

The	For	That	with	know	but
here	on	When	Have	next	we
as	after	good	Make	there	see
Go	Look	Are	Could	is	why
This	who	said	in	come	them
Has	Name	Before	Her	Where	The

To parents — Read the back of a cereal box with your child. Ask him to count the number of capital letters there and write the number next to the cheese.

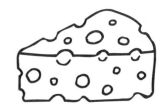

Recognizing Capital Letters

Circle the capital letters that are found on the following items.

Signs and Titles

To parents   Ask your child to find five objects around him that have words containing capital letters.

6

Recognizing Capital Letters

Sing the nursery rhymes below and circle the capital letters that you see.

Nursery Rhymes

I'm a little teapot, short and stout.

Here is my handle and here is my spout.

When I see the teacups, hear me shout.

Tip me over and pour me out.

Row, row, row your boat

Gently down the stream

Merrily, merrily, merrily, merrily

Life is but a dream

To parents Read other rhymes together with your child and have him identify the capital letters in them.

Recognizing Capital Letters

Read the story below and write the capital letters above the small letters that are underlined.

No More Meat!

<u>a</u> dog called <u>t</u>im walked on a bridge over a stream. <u>h</u>e had a piece of meat in his mouth. <u>w</u>hen tim looked into the stream, he saw another dog with a bigger piece of meat. <u>t</u>im wanted another piece of meat. <u>s</u>o he let go of his own piece of meat and jumped at the other piece. <u>b</u>ut it was only his reflection in the water! <u>s</u>adly, <u>t</u>im watched his meat float away from him.

To parents   Have your child identify the capital letters on a page of a storybook, and lead him to see when capital letters are used, i.e. for names and at the beginning of a sentence.

Capitalizing Sentence Beginnings

Note	A sentence begins with a **capital letter**.

Circle the words that show the correct way to begin each sentence.

Squeak!

1. The mouse
the mouse
is looking for food.

2. he finds
He finds
a cracker on the floor.

3. he Eats
He eats
the cracker.

4. Then he
then He
takes a nap.

5. oh No!
Oh no!
He hears a cat!

6. the Mouse
The mouse
runs home fast!

Capitalizing Sentence Beginnings

Draw lines to match the correct capital letter to the beginning of each sentence.

First Day of School

M	we reach school early.
R	the school field is empty.
W	mrs Chan is our new English teacher.
E	everyone stops talking when the principal speaks.
T	ravi's mother waits for him at the school gate.
Y	your sister looks worried.

To parents Ask your child to look through any magazine and find three sentences beginning with 'You'.

Capitalizing Sentence Beginnings

Color the sentence with the correct sentence beginnings.

Harry's Party

1.
| i am at Harry's birthday party. |
| I am at Harry's birthday party. |

2.
| there are girls swimming in the pool. |
| There are girls swimming in the pool. |

3.
| Some boys play football in the garden. |
| some boys play football in the garden. |

4.
| then it starts to rain. |
| Then it starts to rain. |

5.
| We all go into the house. |
| we all go into the house. |

6.
| it is time to cut the cake. |
| It is time to cut the cake. |

To parents Ask your child to look through the newspapers and find three sentences beginning with 'The'.

Capitalizing Sentence Beginnings

Write the beginning words correctly to make a sentence.

Counting Sheep

1.  we read _____ books before bed.

2.  then we _____ hug good night.

3.  my bed _____ is soft and cozy.

4.  the sky _____ has turned dark.

5.  my eyes _____ close.

To parents   Copy a sentence from your child's favorite bedtime book. Have your child circle the capital letter at the beginning.

Capitalizing Sentence Beginnings

Rewrite the sentences below with the correct capital letters for the sentence beginnings.

At the Park

1. i go to the park in the evenings with my father.

   _____

   _____

2. my mother joins us when she can.

   _____

   _____

3. we see many children playing football at the park.

   _____

   _____

4. sometimes we meet our neighbors there.

   _____

   _____

5. they go there to walk their dogs.

   _____

   _____

To parents Ask your child to look through one of his storybooks and find three sentences beginning with 'I'. Have him copy them onto a piece of paper.

Capitalizing Sentence Beginnings

Choose the correct word to fill each blank. Begin with a capital letter. The first one has been done for you.

The Twins

at	but	every	~~jessie~~	unlike	the	she	kevin

1. ___Jessie___ and Kevin are twins.

2. _____ twins like to do different things.

3. _____ likes to play the piano.

4. _____ him, Jessie likes to read.

5. _____ visits the library often to borrow books.

6. _____ day, they go to school by car.

7. _____ school, they are in the same class.

8. _____ they do different things during the breaks.

Capitalizing Names of People and Places

Rewrite the names of the places below with the correct capital letters.

My Neighborhood

1. candy corner

2. lily's lemonade

3. sara fashion

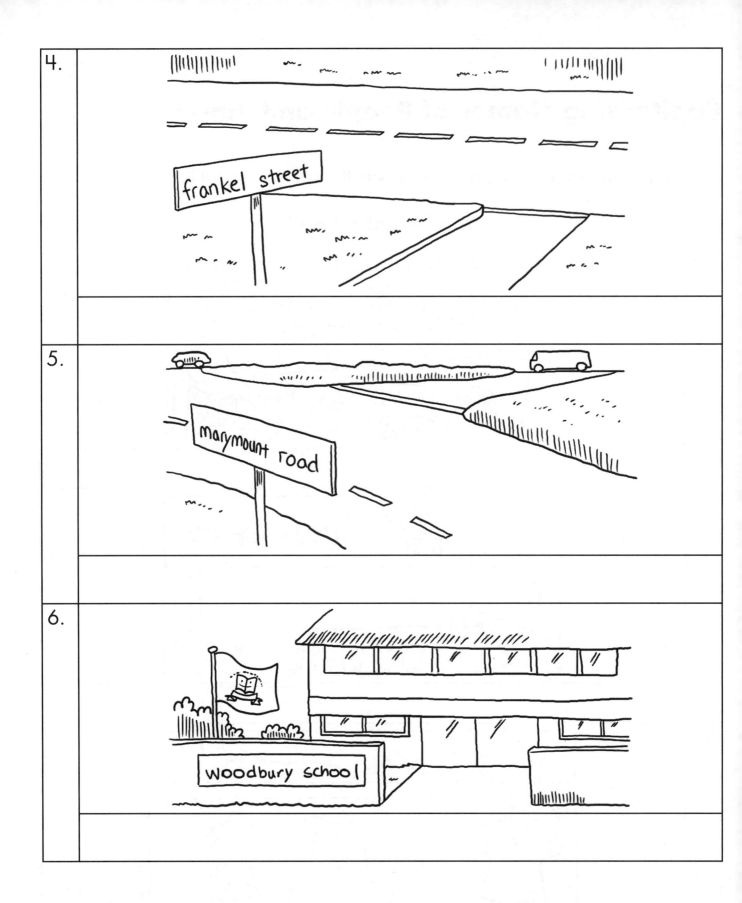

To parents Have your child note down the names of three road signs and one building that he sees when traveling on the way to school the next day.

Capitalizing Names of People and Places

Note	The name of a person or place begins with a capital letter.

Rewrite these name plates with capital letters in the right places. The first one has been done for you.

Knock Knock!

1. dr william

   Dr William _____

2. mr hendricks

   _____

3. mdm agnes

   _____

4. mrs tan

   _____

5. miss vanessa

   _____

6. dr woodsworth

   _____

7. mr xander

   _____

8. miss eileen

   _____

To parents	Ask your child to write the names of three of his school teachers.

Capitalizing Names of People and Places

Rewrite the names and addresses on the envelopes below with the correct capital letters.

Please, Mr Postman

1.

To: paul lee
205C rivervale street
singapore 543205

2.

To: jane martin
100 main street
viper town
NY 12345
USA

3.

To: henry
20 holly road, st. albans
christchurch
new zealand

To parents Check that your child can write his full name and address.

Recognizing Full Stops

Circle the full stops at the end of each sentence.

What Do Animals Give Us?

1. Hens give us eggs.

2. Cows give us milk.

3. Sheep give us wool to make clothes.

4. Bees give us honey.

5. Ducks also give us eggs.

To parents Ask your child to say a sentence on what goats can give us. Write the sentence and ask him to add a full stop at the end.

Recognizing Full Stops

Put a tick (√) beside the sentences that end with full stops.

Animal Helpers

1.

	Horses pull carts and wagons	
	Horses pull carts and wagons.	

2.

	Camels carry people across the hot desert.	
	Camels carry people across the hot desert	

3.

	Dogs help to look after the house	
	Dogs help to look after the house.	

4.

	Elephants help to carry heavy logs.	
	Elephants help to carry heavy logs	

5.

	Donkeys carry people up the mountains	
	Donkeys carry people up the mountains.	

To parents Ask your child to say a sentence about another animal helper. Write the sentence and ask him to add the full stop at the end.

Recognizing Full Stops

Add a full stop (.) to each sentence.

The Night Sky

1. Many things shine in the sky at night

2. The moon looks the brightest

3. It is closest to Earth

4. The stars look like tiny dots

5. They are very far away

6. The sun is a star

7. Planets look like colored stars

8. Their light does not twinkle

9. Shooting stars look like stars that are falling

10. There are many things to see in the night sky

Recognizing Full Stops

Add a full stop (.) at the end of each sentence.

More on Animals

1.
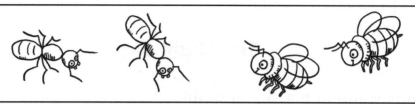

Ants and bees live together in colonies

2.
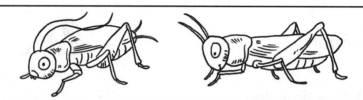

A cricket looks like a grasshopper

3.

Birds have feathers on their bodies

4.

A father goose is called a gander

To parents Write two sentences on any animal without full stops in them. Ask your child to add the full stops.

Punctuating Statements

| Note | A **telling sentence** or statement begins with a **capital letter** and ends with a **full stop**. |

Rewrite each sentence using full stops.

Twinkle, Twinkle Little Star

1. Tonight I saw a star

   _____

2. I saw the star twinkle

   _____

3. It looked like a candle

   _____

4. It was very bright

   _____

5. I made a wish

   _____

6. I hope it comes true

   _____

| To parents | Look for the brightest star in the sky. Ask your child to make a wish and write a sentence about it. Check that it ends with a full stop. |

Punctuating Statements

Rewrite each sentence and add a full stop at the end of it.

A Walk in the Park

1. The sky is blue

    _____

2. The sun is shining brightly

    _____

3. Sally walks happily in the park

    _____

4. She sits under a shady tree

    _____

5. She reads her storybook

    _____

To parents Look through a favorite storybook and have your child copy three sentences onto a piece of paper. Check that each sentence ends with a full stop.

Punctuating Statements

Rewrite each sentence and add a full stop at the end of it.

A Meal at a Café

1. An old woman goes into a café

   _____

2. She sits at a table

   _____

3. She puts her bag on the chair

   _____

4. She orders a piece of cake

   _____

5. She also orders a cup of coffee

   _____

To parents   Ask your child to say three sentences about his favorite café or restaurant. Help him to write them down. Check that each sentence ends with a full stop.

Punctuating Statements

Rewrite each sentence and add a full stop at the end of it.

Taking Care of a Kitten

1. A kitten makes a good pet

   _____

2. You need to take care of it

   _____

3. It needs a place to sleep in

   _____

4. It needs food and drink

   _____

5. It would also love a toy

   _____

Capitalizing/Punctuating Statements

Rewrite each sentence correctly.

Interesting Animal Sounds

1.    the elephant trumpets at its keeper

_____

2.    roosters crow early in the morning

_____

3.    the hens cluck noisily at the farmer

_____

4.    the lion roars noisily in its cage

_____

To parents Ask your child to make the animal sounds in the sentences on this page.

Capitalizing/Punctuating Statements

Note	A **telling sentence** begins with a **capital letter** and ends with a **full stop**.

Rewrite each sentence correctly.

Hop to It!

1. frogs and toads lay eggs

_____

2. the eggs are in the water

_____

3. tadpoles hatch from the eggs

_____

4. the tadpoles grow legs

_____

5. the tadpoles lose their tails

_____

Capitalizing/Punctuating Statements

Rewrite each sentence correctly.

Hop to It Some More!

1. tadpoles become frogs or toods

_____

2. frogs live near water

_____

3. toads live under bushes

_____

4. frogs have wet skin

_____

5. toads have bumpy skin

_____

To parents — Ask your child to write three sentences about a time that he saw a frog or toad. Check that he uses capital letters and full stops correctly.

Capitalizing/Punctuating Statements

Complete the sentences with the given words. Start each sentence with a capital letter and add a full stop at the end of each sentence. The first one has been done for you.

More Animal Sounds

1. <u>Monkeys</u> chatter in the <u>trees</u>.

2. _____ buzz among the _____

3. _____ mew loudly when they

   are _____

4. _____ hoot at _____.

5. _____ dog barks at the _____

To parents Make the sounds of the animals above and ask your child to guess what animals they are.

Date: _____

Capitalizing/Punctuating Statements

Complete the sentences with the given words. Start each sentence with a capital letter and add a full stop at the end of each sentence.

See How The Animals Move!

1. _____ jump from place to _____

2. _____ wriggle in the _____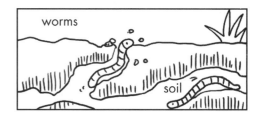

3. _____ prowl when looking for

   _____

4. _____ often pounce on _____

5. _____ hops towards

   _____

To parents Have your child act out the way an animal above moves and try to guess which animal it is.

Writing to Identify People

| **Note** | People could be men, women or children. |

All in the Family

We use these words for people in our family.

| mother | father | sister | brother | uncle | aunt |

In the word square below, find and circle the words given above.

m	b	r	o	t	h	e	r
o	v	f	x	t	q	x	a
t	f	v	a	y	z	v	u
h	s	i	s	t	e	r	n
e	y	v	x	w	h	z	t
r	u	n	c	l	e	e	z
a	v	x	u	y	u	k	r

Writing to Identify People

Note	A person's **occupation** is his or her work or job.

All in a Day's Work

We use these words to refer to some occupations.

doctor	lawyer	teacher	nurse	waiter	singer

In the word square below, find and circle the words given above.

s	l	a	w	y	e	r
i	w	x	y	w	z	z
n	v	a	q	y	v	x
g	q	v	i	x	x	y
e	d	o	c	t	o	r
r	n	u	r	s	e	z
t	e	a	c	h	e	r

Writing to Identify People

More on Work

Here are more words on people's occupations.

| florist | butcher | painter | dentist | baker | pianist | plumber | tailor | photographer |

Write the correct words to match the pictures.

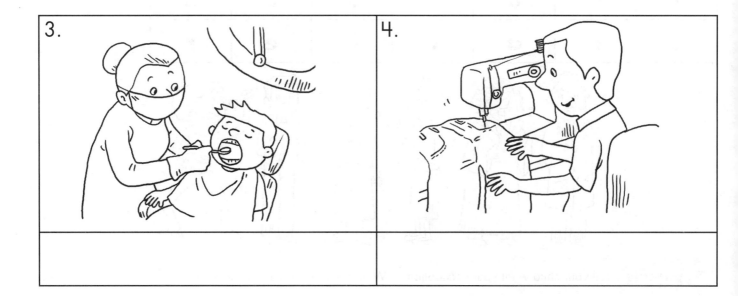

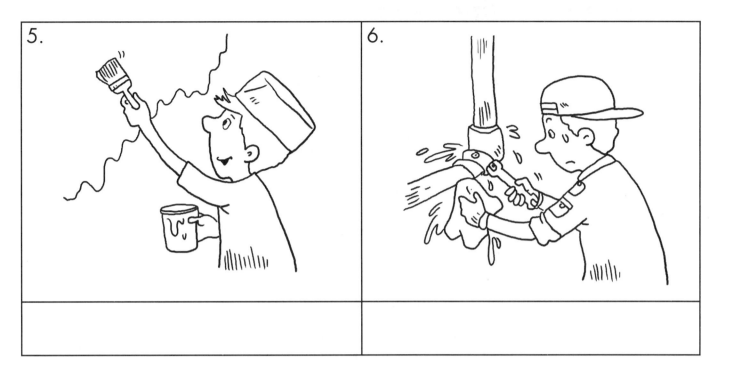

Writing to Identify Places

Note | A place refers to any area or building.

Where am I?

We use these words to refer to places.

park	school	garden	pool	market	toilet

In the word square below, find and circle the words given above.

m	a	r	k	e	t	y	x
g	x	s	c	h	o	o	l
a	p	v	w	q	i	z	x
r	x	o	q	w	l	w	p
d	w	z	o	y	e	x	a
e	x	y	x	l	t	x	r
n	x	q	w	x	z	y	k

To parents | Ask your child to draw a picture of his favorite place.

36

Writing to Identify Places

Where is This Place?

Look at the pictures. Then complete the crossword puzzle. Use the words below to help you.

playground	airport	hotel	museum	stadium	zoo	hospital	classroom

Across

1.

4.

7.

8.

Down

2.

3.

5.

6.

To parents Ask your child to describe his favorite place. Help him to write three sentences on it.

Writing to Identify Places

Use the key below to crack the six codes given and discover the mystery places.

Mystery Places

1	2	3	4	5	6	7	8	9	10
a	b	c	d	e	f	g	h	i	j

11	12	13	14	15	16	17	18	19	20
k	l	m	n	o	p	q	r	s	t

21	22	23	24	25	26
u	v	w	x	y	z

Example:

16	1	18	11
p	a	r	k

1.

6	15	18	5	19	20

2.

16	15	14	4

3.

12	9	2	18	1	18	25

4.

3	1	14	20	5	5	14

5.

15	6	6	9	3	5

6.

19	8	15	16

To parents   Ask your child to name three places that he would like you to take him to. Write their names and read them together.

Writing to Identify Objects

| Note | An **object** refers to something that you can see and touch. |

Things around the House

We use these words to refer to objects.

| pen | shoes | bag | sandwich | bottle | ruler |

In the word square below, find and circle the words given above.

s	a	n	d	w	i	c	h
v	h	v	y	z	x	q	z
b	x	o	p	y	w	w	r
a	y	z	e	w	z	x	u
g	q	w	n	s	q	y	l
w	y	z	x	w	t	x	e
b	o	t	t	l	e	w	r

| To parents | Ask your child to write the names of five objects that he has in his school bag. |

Writing to Identify Objects

Read the clues to help you complete the crossword puzzle. Use these words and pictures to help you.

What am I?

scissors	chair	spoon	table	fork	umbrella	fan	bag

CLUES

Across
2. You fill me up with school books.
4. You use me to cut paper.
5. You do your homework on me.
6. You use me to eat noodles.
7. You sit on me.

Down
1. You need me when you are hot.
3. You open me when it rains.
4. You use me to drink soup.

To parents Ask your child to name and write three objects that he takes with him on a family outing.

Writing to Identify Objects

My Favorite Things

Here are more words used to refer to objects around us. Write the correct words that match the pictures.

flower	apple	umbrella	socks	hat	ball	car	pail	broom

5.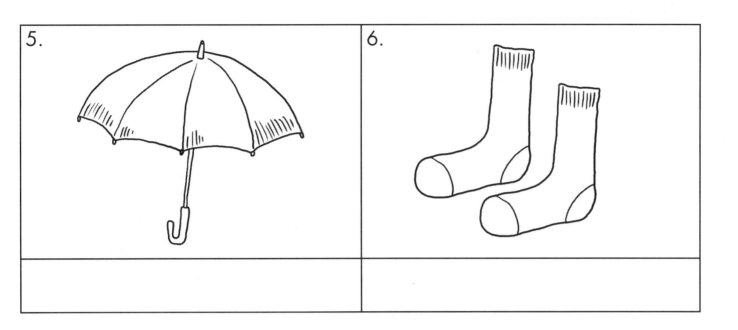

6.

7.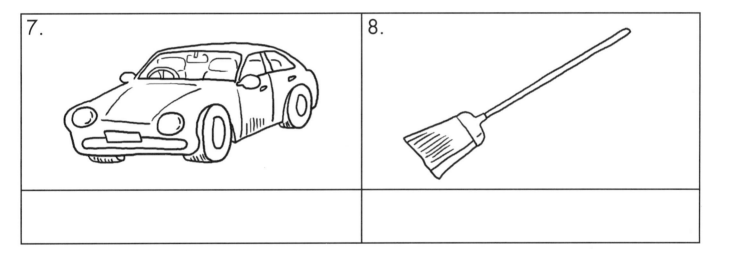

8.

To parents   Ask your child to draw one of his favorite objects and write three sentences about it.

Date: _____

Mini Writing Project 1

Write sentences using the helping words.
Remember to use the correct punctuation marks
and capital letters.

Recap

A sentence begins with
a capital letter and ends
with a full stop.

The name of a person or
place begins with a
capital letter.

1. visit   my uncle   harry

_____

_____

2. my uncle   lives   mackenzie street   australia

_____

_____

3. uncle harry   doctor

_____

_____

4. patients   call him   dr harry smith

_____

_____

5. went   movie world   with   uncle harry

_____

_____

To parents   Find one sentence in a newspaper that contains at least two punctuation marks and two capital letters.

44

Identifying a Sentence

Note	A **sentence** tells a complete idea. It should always make sense.

Patriotic Sentences

Color the flag to show:

RED = sentence   WHITE = not a sentence

★ ★	This is a flag.
	The flag
	The flag has stars.
	The stars
	The stars are white.
	The stripes
	The stripes are red.

And white
The stripes are white.
Blue part
The flag has a blue part.
There are
There are 50 stars.

To parents	Have your child color the star part of the flag with a blue crayon. Then ask him to write a complete sentence about the colorful flag.

Identifying a Sentence

Color each flag that tells a complete thought.

High-Flying Sentences

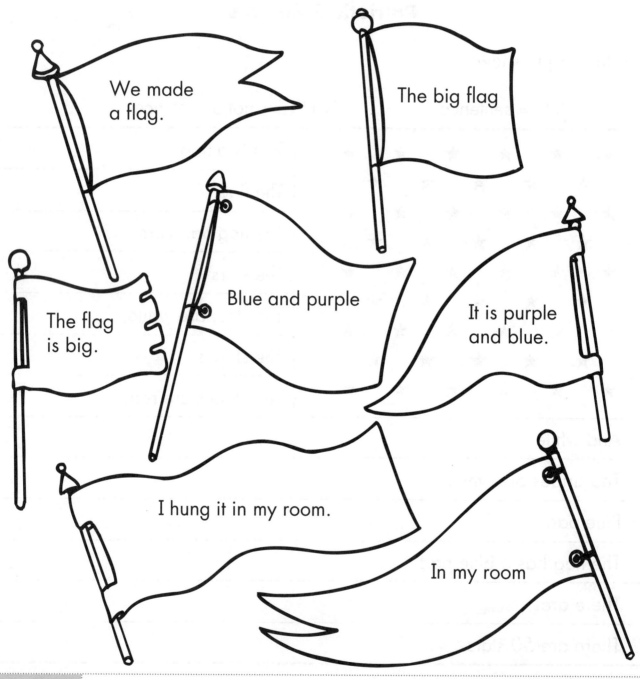

We made a flag.

The big flag

The flag is big.

Blue and purple

It is purple and blue.

I hung it in my room.

In my room

To parents — Ask your child to turn this into a complete sentence: The biggest flag. Check that it begins with a capital letter and ends with a full stop.

Identifying a Sentence

Color the box that contains a sentence.

The Great Outdoors

1.

| I ride a bicycle to school every morning. |
| A bicycle to school. |

2.

| Drives a car to work. |
| My father drives a car to work. |

3.

| My brother likes to sail his boat out to sea. |
| Sail his boat out. |

4.

| My sister rows her canoe down the river. |
| Her canoe down the. |

5.

| To ride on the horse. |
| My mother loves to ride on the horse. |

To parents Ask your child to say a sentence about an outdoor activity. Help him to write the sentence on a piece of paper.

Identifying a Sentence

Color the box that contains a sentence.

What Are They Wearing?

1.

   | A chef wears a tall hat in the kitchen. |
   | Wears a tall hat. |

2.

   | Helmet to protect himself. |
   | A builder wears a hard helmet to protect himself. |

3.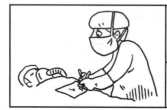

   | A surgeon wears a mask and gloves. |
   | A mask and gloves. |

4.

   | A policeman wears. |
   | A policeman wears a blue uniform. |

5.

   | Mother wears an apron when she cooks. |
   | Apron when she cooks. |

To parents Ask your child to describe what he is wearing. Ask him to write a sentence about his attire.

Sequencing a Sentence

Unscramble the words to make a sentence. Write the sentence below each picture. Finish each picture to match the sentence.

At the Seashore

sailing are boats Five

four have We buckets

Sequencing a Sentence

Unscramble the words to make a sentence. Write the sentence. Do not forget to put a full stop at the end.

In the Rainforest

A hiding jaguar is

blue Some butterflies are

water in jump the Frogs

snakes trees Green hang from

very tall grow The trees

Sequencing a Sentence

Note	A sentence is made up of a **naming part** and an **action part**. Example: <u>Tom</u> is lying in his bed. naming part action part

Rewrite the scrambled sentences correctly.

Sick Tom

1. cannot get up Tom

    _____

2. feels sick He

    _____

3. cannot go He school to

    _____

4. calls doctor His mother for a

_____

5. examines The Tom doctor

_____

6. Tom medicine take to his needs

_____

7. feels He better

_____

8. go Tom school can to

_____

To parents Ask your child to talk about how he feels when he is sick. Have him write a sentence on it. Help him to identify the different parts of the sentence.

Sequencing a Sentence

Rewrite the scrambled sentences correctly.

A New Found Kitty

1. at park the is Darla

    _____

2. hears She mewing sound a

    _____

3. see cannot any She kitten

    _____

4. bush towards the goes Darla

    _____

5. picks the up kitten She

_____

6. takes home it She

_____

7. She it keeps pet as a

_____

Parts of a Sentence: Naming Part

Color the snake that tells the naming part in each sentence below.

Snakes Alive!

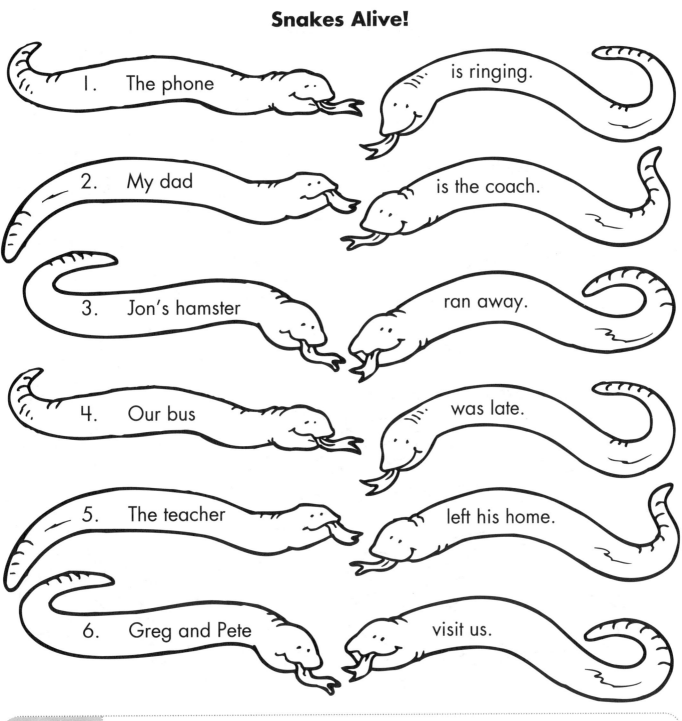

1. The phone   is ringing.
2. My dad   is the coach.
3. Jon's hamster   ran away.
4. Our bus   was late.
5. The teacher   left his home.
6. Greg and Pete   visit us.

To parents Ask your child to write a new sentence for each of the above sentences using a different naming part. Enjoy making funny sentences with him.

57

Parts of a Sentence: Naming Part

Circle the naming part in each sentence below.
Then color the picture to match the sentences.

Slithering Sentences

1. The blue snake is playing with a friend.

2. The yellow snake is climbing a tree.

3. The green snake hides under rocks.

4. The brown snake is swimming.

5. The red snake is hanging on a tree.

6. The purple snake sleeps in trees.

7. The black snake rests on a rock.

8. The orange snake is near an egg.

To parents Ask your child to write a new sentence about the picture in this page, and circle the naming part in the sentence.

58

Parts of a Sentence: Identifying the Action

Note	A sentence has an **action part**. It tells what is happening.

Color the bone that tells the action part in each sentence below.

No Bones About It!

1. The dog | chases the cat.

2. The dog | hides the bone.

3. The dog | plays with a ball.

4. The dog | jumps in the air.

5. The dog | eats a bone.

6. The dog | sleeps on a rug.

To parents Have your child write a new action part to complete the sentence beginning with 'The dog'.

Parts of a Sentence: Identifying the Action

Circle the naming part and underline the action part in each sentence.

Fun at Home

Pauline reads the newspaper.

Lila washes the dishes.

Raymond draws pictures.

Peter watches television.

To parents Have your child write a sentence on an activity that he does at home. Check that he can identify the action part of the sentence.

Parts of a Sentence: Identifying the Action

Circle the naming part and underline the action part in each sentence.

Fun at School

	1. The pupils play soccer.
	2. The teachers have their lunch.
	3. Two girls are running.
	4. The girls are watering the flowers.
	5. The pupils paint the walls.

To parents Talk to your child about what he does in school, and have him write three sentences on these actions. Help him to identify the action parts in the sentences.

Parts of a Sentence: Identifying the Action

Circle the naming part and underline the action part in each sentence.

All Over the World

1. My aunt works in Beijing.

2. Gina lives in Jakarta.

3. We will visit our uncle in India tomorrow.

4. My father is going on a business trip to Paris.

5. Billy mails the letter to his friend in Scotland.

6. Mr Jones bought the book from Sydney.

7. My brother studies in New Zealand.

8. Henry is coming back from Penang today.

To parents Ask your child to tell you about another country he has either visited or heard about. Then have him write two sentences on the activities that have been done there. Help him to identify the action parts in the sentences.

Parts of a Sentence: Completing the Action

Choose the ending that tells what each dog is doing. Remember to use full stops.

Mighty Good Sentences

is eating

is sleeping

is jumping

is barking

1. The white dog _____

2. The gray dog _____

3. The spotted dog _____

4. The striped dog _____

Parts of a Sentence: Completing the Action

Look at the pictures. Use the words below to complete the action part of each sentence.

Cleaning Up

washes	sweeps	folds	wipes	places	makes	irons

1. Mummy _____ all the clean clothes.

2. Billy _____ his dirty bicycle.

3. Amy _____ her toys into the box.

4. My brother _____ the table with a rag.

5. My sister _____ her bed when she wakes up.

6. Nick _____ the floor every day.

To parents | Ask your child to write a sentence on an activity he does to help clean up the house. Check that he can identify the action part.

Parts of a Sentence: Completing the Action

Choose from the given words to match the picture. Then complete the action part for each sentence.

What Can You Do?

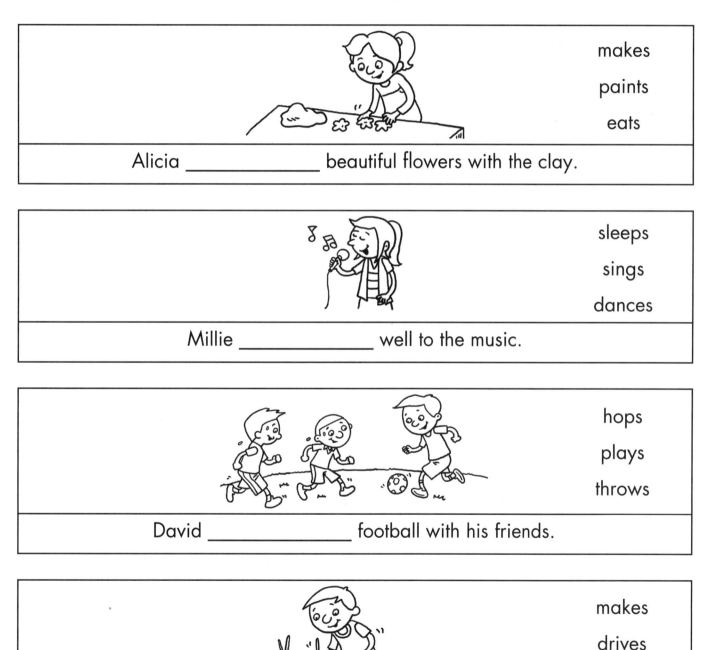

makes

paints

eats

Alicia _____ beautiful flowers with the clay.

sleeps

sings

dances

Millie _____ well to the music.

hops

plays

throws

David _____ football with his friends.

makes

drives

paints

Harvey _____ a picture of a car.

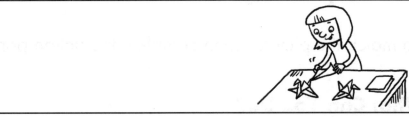

folds

irons

tears

My sister _____ the paper into a paper crane.

cooks

bakes

eats

Mother _____ a chocolate cake for us.

writes

draws

makes

Jake _____ a beautiful parrot on the paper.

dances

walks

sings

May _____ ballet well on stage.

Parts of a Sentence: Determining the Verb

Note	The action part of a sentence begins with a **verb**. The verb tells what the action is.
	Example: We (put) our dirty clothes in the laundry basket.
	The verb 'put' tells what we did to our dirty clothes.

Circle the verb in each sentence.

It's Laundry Time

1. My mother collects all our clothes every morning.

2. She places them into the washing machine.

3. She turns on the washing machine.

4. She puts in a capful of detergent.

5. She takes the clothes out.

6. She hangs the clothes.

To parents   Ask your child to write two verbs related to clothing. Then have him write a sentence for each verb.

Parts of a Sentence: Determining the Verb

Note	Sometimes the verb may contain more than one word.

Underline the verb in each sentence.

Baking Time

1. Grandmother is baking a chocolate cake.
2. Her granddaughter, Annie, is helping her.
3. Both take the eggs, butter, sugar and flour out.
4. Grandmother mixes the sugar and butter together.
5. Annie adds the eggs and flour in.
6. Grandmother stirs the mixture well.
7. Annie pours the mixture into the baking tin.
8. Both place the baking tin into the oven.

To parents	Ask your child to write three verbs on actions that take place in the kitchen. Then have him write a sentence for each verb.

Parts of a Sentence: Determining the Verb

Look at the pictures and fill in the blanks with the verbs below.

What Do You Work As?

arrange	fix	build	take	sew

Nancy, the florist, helps to _____ flowers.

That plumber helps to _____ my neighbour's water pipes.

Mr Chan is the tailor who helps to _____ my clothes.

This photographer loves to _____ pictures of birds.

To parents Ask your child to talk about his favorite occupation. Have him write two sentences on it. Check that he can identify the verb in each sentence.

Parts of a Sentence: Determining the Verb

Note Sometimes the verb does not show action. It still tells **what** is happening.

For example: I the answer.

I am hungry.

Word Bank

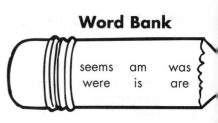

seems   am   was
were   is   are

Choose a verb from the Word Bank to complete each sentence.

Pencil It In

1. I _____ in the first grade.

2. The boys _____ at the movies.

3. The sun _____ hot.

4. Holly _____ tired.

5. We _____ at the park.

To parents Ask your child to form one more sentence for each of the verbs in the Word Bank.

Understanding Sentence Parts

Note A sentence is more interesting when it tells **where** the action is happening.

In each caboose, draw a picture to show where each sentence takes place.

The Caboose

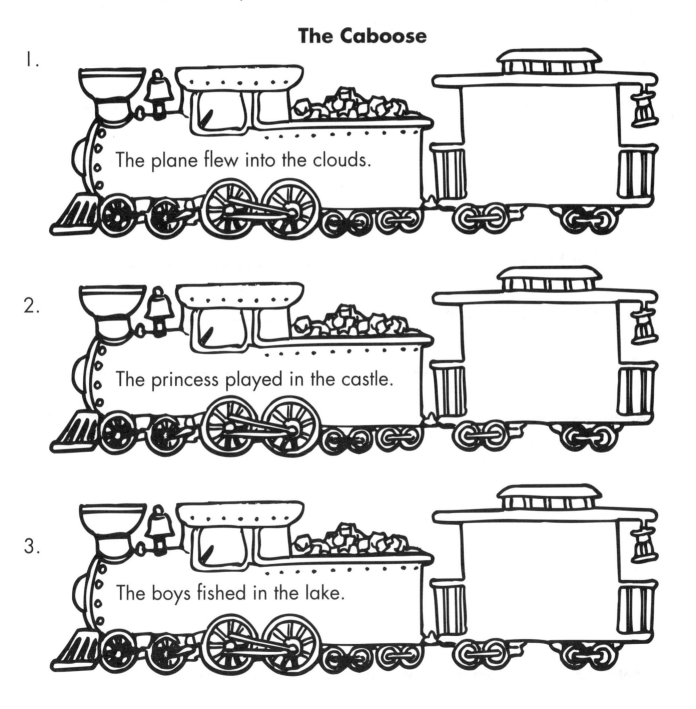

1. The plane flew into the clouds.

2. The princess played in the castle.

3. The boys fished in the lake.

Understanding Sentence Parts

Complete the sentences using the phrases in the box.

Where Does It Happen?

along the running path	in the park	under a tree
in the lake	into the basket	into the air	on the mat

1. Peter cycles _____.

2. His brother jogs _____.

3. His sister reads _____.

4. Their father fishes _____.

5. Their mother packs the fish _____.

6. Their dog jumps _____.

7. Their fat cat lazes _____.

To parents Ask your child to form one more sentence for each of the phrases in the box.

72

Mini Writing Project 2

1. Choose one of the following topics.

- My school
- My family
- My neighborhood

2. List the main people you would talk about for this topic. Some examples are provided below:

father	mother	sister	brother	neighbor
friend	teacher	principal	classmate	

_____   _____

_____   _____

_____   _____

3. Write down some of the things that these people often do. Some examples are provided below:

cook dinner / lunch	read the newpaper	teach a subject
water the flowers	play games	paint a picture

_____   _____

_____   _____

_____   _____

4. Look at the actions you wrote on the previous page. Where do you think they take place? Write down where the action happens. Some examples have been provided:

cook dinner *in the kitchen*   read the newspaper *in the living room*

play games *in the park*   teach English *in the classroom*

_____

_____

_____

_____

5. Now, put everything together. Write sentences to talk about the topic you chose. An example has been provided:

My mother cooks dinner in the kitchen.

_____

_____

_____

_____

_____

_____

To parents Get your child to draw a picture or take a photograph to illustrate each sentence he has written. Compile his writings and pictures into a scrapbook.

Writing Tips

Writing Tip 1: Use capital letters and full stops in statements.

A telling sentence is called a statement. Remember that a statement begins with a capital letter and ends with a full stop. This way, the person who reads your statement knows where it starts and ends.

Look at the two pairs of statements below:
1. The dog sat next to the chair. It was tired.
2. The dog sat next to the chair it was tired.

In the first example, there are two statements. Each statement is a complete thought or idea.

In the second example, it is hard to tell when the first statement ends. The sentence does not make a lot of sense.

Writing Tip 2: Use capital letters in signs, titles and addresses.

You may see capital letters being used in many places. Capital letters are used in signs and titles, for names and in addresses.

Look at an envelope and you will see the capital letters in important words. For example:

To: Mr Paul Michael
    17 Jonas Avenue
    Brighton 50903
    Australia

You should use capital letters when you are referring to a person. For example: Mr Jones, Mrs Jones, Miss Lang or Dr Dixon.

You can also see capital letters on street signs or shop signs. For example: Frankel Avenue, Marymount Road or Main Street.

Remember to include capital letters correctly when you write.

Writing Tip 3: Write complete sentences.

A sentence tells a complete idea. It should have a naming part and an action part. The naming part tells who or what the sentences is about. The action part tells what is happening.

Look at the three examples below:
1. The dog chases the cat.
2. The dog
3. Chases the cat

In the first example, it tells a complete idea. We can tell that the sentence is about the dog and what the dog is doing – chasing the cat. The naming part comes in the first part of the sentence and the action comes after.

The second and third examples do not tell a complete idea.

The second example tells us about the dog. We do not know what happens to the dog because there is no action part.

In the third example, we can tell that something is chasing the cat. We do not know what is chasing the cat.

Remember that when you write a sentence, you must have a naming part and an action part.

Writing Tip 4: Begin the action part with a verb.

When you write the action part of a sentence, begin it with a verb. The verb will tell what the action is.

Look at the example sentences below:
1. The dog chases the cat.
2. My mother washes the dishes.

Which word is the verb in each sentence? The word *chases* and *washes* are verbs. They tell us exactly what the dog and the mother are doing.

Answer Key

Page 5

The, For, That, When, Have, Make, Could, Are, Look, Go, This, Has, Name, Before, Her, Where, The

Page 6

1. P, T, L
2. S, S
3. T, G, O, M
4. M, L
5. C
6. M, B, C
7. N, L
8. E

Page 7

I, H, W, T
R, G, M, L

Page 8

A, T, H, W, T, S, B, S, T

Page 9

1. The mouse
2. He finds
3. He eats
4. Then he
5. Oh no!
6. The mouse

Page 10

M – Mrs Chan is our new English teacher.
R – Ravi's mother waits for him at the school gate.
W – We reach school early.
E – Everyone stops talking when the principal speaks.
T – The school field is empty.
Y – Your sister looks worried.

Page 11

1. I am at Harry's birthday party.
2. There are girls swimming in the pool.
3. Some boys play football in the garden.
4. Then it starts to rain.
5. We all go into the house.
6. It is time to cut the cake.

Page 12

1. We read
2. Then we
3. My bed
4. The sky
5. My eyes

Page 13

1. I go to the park in the evenings with my father.
2. My mother joins us when she can.
3. We see many children playing football at the park.
4. Sometimes we meet our neighbors there.
5. They go there to walk their dogs.

Page 14

1. Jessie
2. The
3. Kevin
4. Unlike
5. She
6. Every
7. At
8. But

Pages 15–16

1. Candy Corner
2. Lily's Lemonade
3. Sara Fashion
4. Frankel Street
5. Marymount Road
6. Woodbury School

Page 17

1. Dr William
2. Mr Hendricks
3. Mdm Agnes
4. Mrs Tan
5. Miss Vanessa
6. Dr Woodsworth
7. Mr Xander
8. Miss Eileen

Page 18

1. Paul Lee
   205C Rivervale Street
   Singapore 543205
2. Jane Martin
   100 Main Street
   Viper Town
   NY 12345
   USA
3. Henry
   20 Holly Road, St. Albans
   Christchurch
   New Zealand

Page 19

1. Hens give us eggs.
2. Cows give us milk.
3. Sheep give us wool to make clothes.
4. Bees give us honey.
5. Ducks also give us eggs.

Page 20
1. bottom 2. top
3. bottom 4. top
5. bottom

Page 21
Review that a full stop (.) is added at the end of each sentence.

Page 22
Review that a full stop (.) is added at the end of each sentence.

Page 23
1. Tonight I saw a star.
2. I saw the star twinkle.
3. It looked like a candle.
4. It was very bright.
5. I made a wish.
6. I hope it comes true.

Page 24
1. The sky is blue.
2. The sun is shining brightly.
3. Sally walks happily in the park.
4. She sits under a shady tree.
5. She reads her storybook.

Page 25
1. An old woman goes into a café.
2. She sits at a table.
3. She puts her bag on the chair.
4. She orders a piece of cake.
5. She also orders a cup of coffee.

Page 26
1. A kitten makes a good pet.
2. You need to take care of it.
3. It needs a place to sleep in.
4. It needs food and drink.
5. It would also love a toy.

Page 27
1. The elephant trumpets at its keeper.
2. Roosters crow early in the morning.
3. The hens cluck noisily at the farmer.
5. The lion roars noisily in its cage.

Page 28
1. Frogs and toads lay eggs.
2. The eggs are in the water.
3. Tadpoles hatch from the eggs.
4. The tadpoles grow legs.
5. The tadpoles lose their tails.

Page 29
1. Tadpoles become frogs or toads.
2. Frogs live near water.
3. Toads live under bushes.
4. Frogs have wet skin.
5. Toads have bumpy skin.

Page 30
2. Bees, flowers.
3. Kittens, hungry.
4. Owls, night.
5. The, stranger.

Page 31
1. Frogs, place.
2. Worms, soil.
3. Lions, food.
4. Cats, rats.
5. The rabbit, the carrots.

Page 32

m	b	r	o	t	h	e	r
o	v	f	x	t	q	x	a
t	f	v	a	y	z	v	u
h	s	i	s	t	e	r	n
e	y	v	x	w	h	z	t
r	u	n	c	l	e	e	z
a	v	x	u	y	u	k	r

Page 33

s	l	a	w	y	e	r
i	w	x	y	w	z	z
n	v	a	q	y	v	x
g	q	v	i	x	x	y
e	d	o	c	t	o	r
r	n	u	r	s	e	z
t	e	a	c	h	e	r

Pages 34–35
1. butcher 2. pianist
3. dentist 4. tailor
5. painter 6. plumber
7. florist 8. photographer

78

Page 36

m	a	r	K	e	f	y	x
g	x	s	c	h	o	o	l
a	p	v	w	q	i	z	x
r	x	o	q	w	l	w	p
d	w	z	o	y	e	x	a
e	x	y	x	l	t	x	r
n	x	q	w	x	z	y	k

Page 37
1. airport
2. playground
3. hospital
4. classroom
5. museum
6. hotel
7. stadium
8. zoo

Pages 38–39
1. forest
2. pond
3. library
4. canteen
5. office
6. shop

Page 40

s	a	n	d	w	i	c	h
v	h	v	y	z	x	q	z
b	x	o	p	y	w	w	r
a	y	z	e	w	z	x	u
g	q	w	n	s	q	y	l
w	y	z	x	w	t	x	e
b	o	t	t	l	e	w	r

Page 41
1. fan
2. bag
3. umbrella
4. scissors
5. table
6. fork
7. chair

Pages 42–43
1. ball
2. flower
3. pail
4. apple
5. umbrella
6. socks
7. car
8. broom

Page 44
Answers will vary. Check that names and sentences begin with a capital letter, and sentences end with a full stop.

Page 45
RED:
This is a flag.
The flag has stars.
The stars are white.
The stripes are red.
The stripes are white.
The flag has a blue part.
There are 50 stars.

Page 46
COLOR:
We made a flag.
The flag is big.
It is purple and blue.
I hung it in my room.

Page 47
1. I ride a bicycle to school every morning.
2. My father drives a car to work.
3. My brother likes to sail his boat out to sea.
4. My sister rows her canoe down the river.
5. My mother loves to ride on the horse.

Page 48
1. A chef wears a tall hat in the kitchen.
2. A builder wears a hard helmet to protect himself.
3. A surgeon wears a mask and gloves.
4. A policeman wears a blue uniform.
5. Mother wears an apron when she cooks.

Page 49
Five boats are sailing.
We have four buckets.

Page 50
A jaguar is hiding.
Some butterflies are blue.
Frogs jump in the water.
Green snakes hang from trees.
The trees grow very tall.

Pages 51–52
1. Tom cannot get up.
2. He feels sick.
3. He cannot go to school.
4. His mother calls for a doctor.
5. The doctor examines Tom.
6. Tom needs to take his medicine.
7. He feels better.
8. Tom can go to school.

Page 53–54
1. Darla is at the park.
2. She hears a mewing sound.
3. She cannot see any kitten.
4. Darla goes towards the bush.
5. She picks up the kitten.
6. She takes it home.
7. She keeps it as a pet.

Page 55
1. Harry
2. Sally
3. Ronny
4. Violet

Page 56
1. My family
2. My mother
3. My sister
4. My father
5. I
6. My father
7. My mother
8. We

Page 57
1. The phone
2. My dad
3. Jon's hamster
4. Our bus
5. The teacher
6. Greg and Pete

Page 58
1. The blue snake
2. The yellow snake
3. The green snake
4. The brown snake
5. The red snake
6. The purple snake
7. The black snake
8. The orange snake
Review that the colors match the sentences.

Page 59
1. chases the cat
2. hides the bone
3. plays with a ball
4. jumps in the air
5. eats a bone
6. sleeps on a rug

Page 60
1. Pauline reads the newspaper.
2. Lila washes the dishes.
3. Raymond draws pictures.
5. Peter watches television.

Page 61
1. The pupils play soccer.
2. The teachers have their lunch.
3. Two girls are running.
4. The girls are watering the flowers.
5. The pupils paint the walls.

Page 62
1. My aunt works in Beijing.
2. Gina lives in Jakarta.
3. We will visit our uncle in India tomorrow.
4. My father is going on a business trip to Paris.
5. Billy mails the letter to his friend in Scotland.
6. Mr Jones bought the book from Sydney.

7. My brother studies in New Zealand.
8. Henry is coming back from Penang today.

Page 63
1. is jumping.
2. is barking.
3. is eating.
4. is sleeping.

Page 64
1. folds
2. washes
3. places
4. wipes
5. makes
6. sweeps

Pages 65–66
1. makes
2. sings
3. plays
4. paints
5. folds
6. bakes
7. draws
8. dances

Page 67
1. My mother collects all our clothes every morning.
2. She places them into the washing machine.
3. She turns on the washing machine.
4. She puts in a capful of detergent.
5. She takes the clothes out.
6. She hangs the clothes.

Page 68
1. Grandmother is baking a chocolate cake.
2. Her granddaughter, Annie, is helping her.
3. Both take the eggs, butter, sugar and flour out.
4. Grandmother mixes the sugar and butter together.
5. Annie adds the eggs and flour in.
6. Grandmother stirs the mixture well.
7. Annie pours the mixture into the baking tin.
8. Both place the baking tin into the oven.

Page 69
1. arrange
2. fix
3. sew
4. take

Page 70
1. am
2. are/were
3. is/was
4. is/was
5. are/were

Page 71
Review that the pictures match the sentences.

Page 72
1. in the park
2. along the running path
3. on the mat
4. in the lake
5. into the basket
6. into the air
7. under a tree

Pages 73–74
Answers will vary.

80